Copyright 2020 Ashley Ikwueme

No part of this publication may be reproduced in whole or in part, or stored in a retrieval system, or transmitted in any form or by any means, electronic, mechanical, photocopying, recording, or otherwise, without written permission of the publisher.

Being Free Publishing, Inc

Atlanta, Georgia

770-905-2517

My Beloved

Finding Love within yourself

(Beloved/Be-Loved)

CONTENTS

I. The Journey (Walk Your Journey)

II. The Promise

III. A Broken Heart

IV. Failure Reality

V. Baby Steps

VI. The Pause Effect (Wasted Time, Wasted People)

    I. Surrender

    II. Reshape (Building Back Up)

    III. Reverse the Curse

    IV. Hidden Truth (Pain)

    V. Birthing

    VI. Be-loved

INTRODUCTION

Writing this book is literally a Journey on its own. To be in a place of complete silence and solitude with the Lord, has been challenging. I got so consumed with the doing I forgot about the being. Being free, being happy, truly being me. Due to living in the day by day it's hard to understand the being...what is it to be myself? This is a place where I am literally reading, writing, listening, and watching Jesus. Yet you would think that the season I am in is a part of my daily life but nope. I'm here to tell you that I'm just as messed up as you. It's crazy though, because my soul longs and cries for these deep moments with God but to realize the stillness of who He is, is quite uncomfortable at times. I pray this book inspires you, lifts you up, and helps you continue to live out your purpose in life during this season of singleness. This is your time to shine and to fall in love with the best version of you. No! you will not be perfect but learn to walk in all your imperfections knowing that God has you where you are for his purpose and when you walk into wifehood you will be ready to take on the mantle of a wife because you grew in the season of a single woman. For the men who read this know that you too have purpose during your single season, although it may look different from mine, know that you too have to prepare your life to carry the mantle of a kingdom husband. Growing in your single season will open doors for you to lead your family into the presence of heaven when you become a husband. Let's all continue to grow in the place we are in our lives and leave with the best outcome. Continue to pray over your life and watch as miracles begin to come as you transform into a strong healthy person mentally, physically, emotionally, and spiritually.

CHAPTER ONE

The Journey

We all look at our end results, forget the beginning, and overlook that path that we are on. Like all things, remembering where you came from is essential. Focusing on the journey that you are currently on helps us grow. Growth will happen and growth is happening, I believe that as you read this book you will grow, I believe that as you accept this season of your life you will become free and at peace. Let my journey help your journey. Let your journey be a testimony to how good God is and how much he loves you in every season of your life. By the end of this book when I leave you with a prayer, I pray that you view your single season as a blessing. That you see yourself as the wonderful woman or man of God that you're created to be. Your journey is as important as mine. My journey started off when I was unable and incapable of doing what I just did. Writing. If you told me five years ago, I would write a book I would have laughed in your face. Never did I ever see this coming. However, my journey started differently than expected. The journey started when I felt like the lord spoke to me about someone else. For many like myself it is easier to help someone else out of their struggles or help them believe in themselves before we do it for ourselves.

I am just that kind of person and the lord knows how much giving of myself was more natural to me then looking into the mirror. A few years back while I was in college, I felt like the lord had challenged me to start writing. Everyone talked about how journaling is an open doorway to record what the lord is doing in our lives. However, this was not just about the good and bad days. I heard him say write but write for her. Who is her? I wondered then I looked up and saw a dear friend of mine sitting in front of me, and I was like 'her God?" it's not that I did not love her but why would I write for her? Little did I know how much writing for her was going to entail and change me. Though the challenge seemed hard and out of me I was obedient and got a book and began writing. There were many times it was hard, and I did not want to write but I did my best to keep going. This challenge was definitely out of my comfort zone. For two years I wrote in this journal all kinds of things. Whatever I felt the lord spoke to me, I wrote. Whatever prayer she needed, I prayed, and I wrote. For two years I took time to pour into someone else through prayer and writing. Little did I know the self-impact I would get out of that. Now I get to not only grow but I get to also pray for you as I did for her journey. If it takes me two years, it's worth two years of God's covering in your life.

I am not a writer. I repeat I am not a writer. If any of you know me, you know writing is not my strong point. In fact, it may be my weakest. I have always struggled with reading and writing since I was a kid. I see things in a dyslexic way and all my letters get mixed up. Some days I forget how to spell my own name. Let's not even talk about grammar. I'm sure if you read this before it gets edited you would cry at all my grammar mishaps. I know crazy right to think I can't write yet I wrote a book. That just shows how good God is and how we can do anything through him (Philippians 4:13). He took my weakness turned it to a strength and used my journey of growth for my friend to one day challenge myself and now it's to challenge you! This journey not only helped me become a book writer. It also helped me become an independent single girl. This book shines the light on the journey, the truth, the highs and lows, and most of all the blessing of being in your single season. And being in the season that the lord has you in. Let this help you grow and learn to appreciate the outcomes of where you are at currently in your life. Yes, there is an end goal but first we must start, then we must evaluate where we are before we begin moving forward. Let's start your journey and get you to become the best version of you.

CHAPTER TWO

The Promises

The promises of god are yes and amen (2 Corinthians 1;20)

Seek first the kingdom of God (Matthew 6:33)

Walking in God's promises sounds a lot easier than sometimes done. It feels good to know that you have a promise over your life. However, are you willing to fight for that promise? We hear all the time; I am waiting for my promise from God but what does that look like? Are we literally just sitting around and waiting for God to come through or is there more to waiting on the promises of God. As a single person I think at times we misunderstand what waiting for "the one" looks like. In my own waiting I found myself falling for this unrealistic standard of waiting as well. Where did this idea even come from? What's the right way to wait? What am I really waiting for? All questions I found myself asking and trying to figure out in this "waiting" season. But what if I told you waiting was simply being. Being who you were intended to be all along. If we look back at the story of Adam and Eve, we can see how Adam never really waited for Eve. He was busy! Adam was busy working, naming animals, walking and talking with God, swimming in the pure and clean sea. He was busy living his best life. Adam never really stopped to wait for Eve. God in all his love and grace saw that Adam needed a companion and a helper. Then he put him to rest, in that resting time He then brought Adam his Eve. So, what does that say for us who are "waiting"? Are we really out here working, getting things done, enjoying life, staying busy or are we just sitting around searching for "the one"? If you are restless then you're not where you need to be. Come on now let's be honest with ourselves. We are big boys and girls, let's not just hear what we want to hear. If we are so stressed out in search for "making my life look perfect" then we are not doing what God wants us to do. This time of your life is to do God's will for your life. To be that amazing teacher, lawyer, mother, friend whatever it is God has placed before you this is your time to work and Stewart that thing well. Chase after your dreams and be your best self, live your best life. Then and only then will you come to a place of rest within yourself and little will you know that "promise" will come to pass.

Let me give you another great example that most of us know. How about the story or Ruth and Boaz. I know many of us christans know this story especially women. Why? Because we always say phrases like I'm waiting on my Boaz. Girl let me tell you something we do Ruth dirty when we talk about waiting for our Boaz. If I was her, I would be upset with all the women that follow after me if they thought my story was to encourage them to wait on a man. Once again please hear my heart I am not saying the desires and promise to have a husband is bad. No, it's great! Its godly! It is full of purpose. But our perspective in which we wait for him needs to be shifted. Ruth did not go into that field with makeup on her face and a cute outfit waiting for Boaz to walk by. She was working and working hard. The very purpose why Ruth was even in that field had nothing to do with Boaz but everything to do with her life and her family. Ruth was on a mission, but her mission was not her man. Her mission was her life and she got blessed with her man along the way. Don't believe me, take a look at that story. You can find it in the book of Ruth. It's only 4 chapters, take a look at Ruth and see it from a different perspective.

Let me give you one more story before we transition into deeper things. My story my promise. I did not grow up wanting to be a wife in fact this girl never wanted to get married or have kids. I know some of you may be saying so ask how you can even write a book about marriage if you did not want it. Well let me tell you why I was so against getting married, it's simple I was broken. I grew up not seeing what a godly marriage looked like. Not to say that my parents did not try. I was just too young to grasp what may have been good and all I remembered was the moments in which they were bad. My young undeveloped mind had a hard time knowing what marriage was but in my fantasy idea it was all about being happy 24/7. So, where did my want come from, heaven! It was not long after I got saved did the lord begin to do a work on my heart about everything, including marriage. The lord had to do a work for me through all my pain and showed me how marriage was his will and how marriage was his design. It was not long after that revelation that he told me about my husband. "My promise" the lord began to fill my heart with dreams and vision of this amazing man I would one day marry. He spoke to me about his character, the mantel he would carry, and the ministry we would uphold together. In that moment my heart was so full of hope and wonder of who this man could be. But it took me time to realize that my perspective of marriage had to change from living in this fairytale that had not yet come to being who God wanted Ashley to be. I did not know I would take the next few years to continue working and shaping who I was as a leader, sister, and friend. My focus was not about my husband but everything God called me to be.

My husband will just be a bonus to my life bringing in a new chapter of purpose, while I already lived in full purpose.

Does your life have purpose yes! Is your desire to be a husband or wife Godly amen! The promises of God are yes and amen (2 Corinthians 1:20) and you will see your desires come to pass, but don't get lost in seeking only what you desire, get lost in seeking out your purpose. Who are you made to be. How are you working, can you truly say your focus is not building yourself and loving yourself in this season or are we still lost in thinking about whether he or she finds you attractive? Is it hard yes, I know it is. I am right there with you. However, we need to renew our minds and shift our focus to the right things. If I know one thing about God, he always keeps his promises so I have no doubt in my mind that the desire he placed in my heart and yours to be a spouse will come true. However, what I also know is that he called us to be the hands and feet of Jesus and no matter what that looks like in your life, know that when you walk out your purpose you promise is right behind you.

CHAPTER THREE

A Broken Heart

I know I said this book was about you, and it still is. However, this chapter is important to me that you know that I am not just some girl telling you what to do, but understanding the walk that you're in. I too have been where you are and had to learn how to seek God's voice and trust him in my walk. I learned how to trust him and want him in his will and timing. Your life is in God's hands and my prayer is that you let him teach you.

Most teens after graduating high school get excited to venture off into the real world and experience all the things college has to offer. The excitement to try new things like clubs, bars, new people that we meet, and even new relationships sounds so tempting. That was me honestly when thinking about it all, however like I said unlike most I took a different route. In 2011 after graduating high school I decided to Go to bible school, and let me tell you there were no clubs, no bars, and no boys I had any interest in. so why go to bible school you may ask? Well I was saved! Not saying all saved people have to go to bible school. I just loved the lord. I had got saved around 16 so at 18 when deciding to go to school the idea of losing my faith was not acceptable to *me. All the things that came with normal college just did not seem like enough for me just to be honest. Yes, I had moments where I desired those things, but I wanted more than that. Let me just say that GOING TO BIBLE SCHOOL DOES NOT take away the desires of the world. Your heart and your mind does not one day wake up and say ok I do not want to go parties any more or I don't wanna — (fill in the blank) just like anything that had to do with my walk with God I had to choose to live a life of surrender and obedience. Let me tell you surrendering your life to God is so worth it and also so hard to do at times. But I had to make a decide who I wanted to serve. Sounds churchy right? But it's true. I had to make up in my mind what I wanted my life to be. Even though I chose to give up some of the things that my flesh wanted like being wild and free! It did not mean I did not have struggles. I faced many challenges during the years including losing myself in a relationship. Moments came that helped outweigh the bad. Such as friends and leadership that changed my perspective. But it did not mean your girl had it all together, I still don't have it all together.*

Though living in my best imperfect self, I loved what I did when It came to ministry. One thing about being involved in a ministry school was having the opportunity to experience different forms of leadership. Due to my lack of knowing where I wanted to serve, I allowed myself to keep an open mind and served everywhere. Little did I know that where I choose to serve opened doors for me that shifted my life. One ministry I was highly active in was kids. I have always had a love for babies and little ones. In fact, that's all I wanted to do was be a teacher for them early stages. So, hey why not do what you love most at a school that trains you for it. While serving in this ministry I was able to meet many different families and kids. Little did I know that one of the families I would meet would become like my own during my first year of school. A few months later a door opened where I would begin serving in the outreach ministry for the young adults. This was not what I wanted nor what I felt called to however I decided to serve anyway, and little did I know I would fall in love with service outside of the four walls of a church building. Little did I know how connections would come from all over.

Let's go back to kids' ministry, like I said I loved it and I loved the opportunity I gained from it. I just felt like I was on top of my game and I was making a difference in the lives of these kids. One family I met had these beautiful chocolate baby twins. They were so cute and so loving. I instantly fell in love with them. I just felt like I knew them for so long even though they were only 7 months old. I cared for them with many other children at the time, but they clung to me like family. So, week after week I got to love on them and see all the kids grow over time. There is just something about seeing the kids you teach start to pick up on the lessons and use them.in their lives. One day I had both of the twins in my lap holding them and rocking them to sleep before they got picked up, singing this sweet song to them as they fell asleep. As their mother came to pick them up, she got a glimpse of my singing which may I say is not the best out there. As she gathered their things we began to talk and it just felt so natural, we started sharing things about life and dreams like we knew each other forever. That one moment open the door to a great friendship.

Week after week I spent time with the kids but also with the mom. Now this is where the plot twist comes for this whole story. The mom let's say her name was Jill. Jill was a mother to many, but little did I know she was also the mother to the man I would call my first love. Remember how I said I started serving in the young adult's outreach ministry. Well here is that story. So here I am still this hungry for God, still loving kids but also in this open-minded place. Remember how I said that I was open to do almost anything, well I did, not only did I work with kids I worked with outreach and on Tuesday nights I was always ready to go be the hands and feet. Every Tuesday I would get on a church bus with a few other people to ride into the surrounding neighborhoods and pick up people wanting to come to church. This ministry was beyond amazing to me, a passion I never knew I had. Seeing people get on the bus week after week just to come hear about Jesus was everything. Even though let's be honest at times people only came for a quick getaway or even food but who cares they heard about the God who created them and the man who died for them, so it was all good to me. Week after week I got on the bus and rode out, it was not long till I realized that I was not the only person consistently riding the bus. Here was this guy who rode the bus every week just like me. I didn't even really know him or talk to him much outside of us riding the bus, but I loved that we got to do it together. Every week was the same until one day something changed. I don't know what it was, but he must have had a bad day and out of nowhere he just opened up to me about what was going on. Needless to say, that day began the day of our friendship.

Our friendship grew quick there was just this spark that just made sense. We talked a little more and more as time went on. The girl he was talking to at the time I found out that the advice shared with her was for him. It was crazy but it also made us bond. Then remember the woman "Jill" come to find out Jill was his mom well, his adoptive mom but still him mom. Everything just clicked in this weird way. It felt crazy but also like destiny. As I left school for winter break, I truly felt in my heart that I liked him. But at the time I did not even want to be married. So here I was really liking this guy and really feeling like the lord brought him to me but for what I had no idea. As time went on, we dated and quickly broke up. I found myself pushing him away and doing harmful things out of fear. I was just in a broken place I had not realized I was in. It broke my heart when we were no longer together, but it also opened my eyes to see that I had work that needed to be done inside of me. In that season I saw how my past affected who I was, I also saw how I had desired to one day be a wife, a desire I had never had until then. So, where does this broken heart come from? It came from my pain, my past and my misunderstanding of what I truly desired. Brokenness truly showed its face when I lost this relationship, brokenness came when I lost my friend, brokenness came when I got suspended from school. Brokenness was more than a feeling it was what I had to overcome. You too can overcome brokenness in your life.

CHAPTER FOUR

False reality

What do we think marriage is really about. We think it's all about the love that's in the air, and the cute pictures couples take together. Let me stop you dead in your tracks before you begin to daydream. Marriage is not all about that. In fact, that's just the icing on the cake. Too many times we get lost in this Disney idea of your princess or prince thinking that one you need to be waiting around or looking for your prince or that your life is focused on requiring the woman in need. No, no we need to toss that mindset away. As much as I love Disney and I love all things about the princess, this mindset of what a relationship should look like in a fairytale ideality is unhealthy.

 God did not intend for us to rebel to find love. Yes, I said rebel show me one love story that we look up to that does not have some crazy unrealistic point of view. I mean even our movies are not all truth. I'm not saying finding love is not magical or not having these grand moments of passion, but that's what they are moments. Too many times we get lost in thinking that the moments we see in movies are the lifelong responsibilities of marriage. Nope we are wrong! The lifelong commitment come when the moments of dancing in the rain fade or the moments of that wonderful first long kiss is gone. I mean think about it do you know many times the actor and actress had to rehearse a kissing Scene for that five seconds of passion in a movie. I am not one hundred percent sure, but I have listened to many stories of how it was awkward and how they had to run the screen over multiple times. We think boom there just on camera and the love is just authentic. Come on y'all let's be real, we know that no one just hops on film and everything looks perfect I mean how many times do you take a picture before you even post one on Instagram. If it takes you to take 100 selfies before you like one, to even post on social media how many times do you think the actor and actress ran through their kissing scene.

Now I don't want to discourage you guys and gals. I'm not saying love won't ever look like that. I'm not saying you won't have moments where it feels all like a movie and a dream. It will and you will have those moments but just know that they are moments. Moments to love and look forward to but what will you do once the moments pass. I'm telling you this because I want you to have a solid foundation in your relationship. I want you to be so strong in who you are that you don't get lost in a daydream. You have so much more to offer than something you just saw on tv. You have your intelligence, your passions, your spiritual maturity and so much more to offer in your relationship than just the moments. If you can't talk to each other then what's the point? That's all I just want you to see. See yourself as more than.

Shifting our perspective from a dream to reality can be hard at times I know I had moments when it was hard for me. I to found myself daydreaming about my prince but what was I really bringing to the table? I had to offer more than just a pretty smile. So, once I shifted my perspective, I then began to see myself as so much more. This single season was about me becoming my best me and it's about you becoming your best you. Like I said before you're not becoming anything for anyone but yourself, you're not even doing it for me this is all about YOU!!! Remember to repeat this daily. This is about you! This season, this life, this book, it's all about you finding and loving your best you. You are living in your purpose!

CHAPTER FIVE

Baby Steps

When a child begins to walk, they go through a process of stretching. Learning how to stand, learning how to trust, learning how to move in the right direction. Growing into the next phase of our development can at times seem challenging but are very beneficial for our growth.

Growth is not meant to feel comfortable, in fact; it's one of the most uncomfortable things we experience. You may not remember the pain you felt in the moments of learning how to walk but did you do it in the moments when you were getting taller? How about in the moments when your body hit puberty? I don't know about you, but I know I felt all my growth pains. I remember the pain of literally transforming into the new version of me. In this Season there is no difference the pain of growth is inevitable but necessary. Growth pains are meant for us to do just that, grow! They are set up so we can learn how to trust, and we can learn how to take baby steps. It's all a big set up for a stronger and better version of you.

Ask yourself what growth pains are you feeling in this season? What baby steps is the Lord speaking to you about? For any of us I would be bold enough to say that the steps we are working *on are self. We have gotten into a routine of living for every and anything but self. We think too much of what others think, we work for the approval of man and get lost in the fairytale of it all. If we are honest, we don't even show the real self to anyone we just give them the fake moments we call reality. I can honestly say I have fallen subject to this in my own life. However, Brothers and sisters our baby steps begin with us. Not us as in you and another but us as in you and you. You are yourself with your reflection of you and your God. When we hear baby steps if we are honest, we are already looking for this 3-step process to becoming a good wife or to conquer whatever your purpose is for more. What if I told you there are not three steps, but many steps and the goal is not a title but an identity. This life is full of baby steps, in every season where we are growing and stretching our internal selves to walk externally. It's painful and ongoing. It's full of strength and purpose!*

Here's the thing about baby steps, once we take our first our second step is so much easier. It may not feel easy, but the hardest part is the first step. But let me continue to be real with you just because you took a step or two won't mean you won't fall. The beginning steps are the hardest but you're still learning, you're still growing. So, let's do two things; one I want you to think of the season you're in right now. No matter what it is, think of what you need to take baby steps in. Then ask yourself this: Have I taken the first step? If not, come on, you got this. If you have this, the next part is for you. Celebrate yourself! Go ahead, give yourself that pat on the back or that hand clap. I'm for real doing it right now. We have forgotten what it means to celebrate our little wins and our baby steps. It's hard when a baby takes its first steps, so we celebrate them so why not celebrate your steps you take in life now. Whether you're reading this book for self-love or becoming a wife or even if it's just a fresh read you my friend took a step today and that deserves all the celebration. The second part of this is it's ok when you fall. Falling is as hard as taking those first steps but falling means winning. Ashley, how can you say this because when you're down the only way left to go is up. You're in a growing place and like a plant you're planted down to come back up. So, falling will happen but so will rising. So, if you fail during this season don't beat yourself up but rise back up into the stronger you, the bolder you. One motivational speech I love listening to is Denzel Washington's speech on failing. He says "if I'm going to fall, I want to fall forward "falling cam and it will happen it's all about the direction you choose to fall. And if you choose to get back up again. Ask yourself this am I down? Have I fallen? And am I ready to get back up? The get up is stronger than the fall down. And just as a baby needs to be consistent in stepping and falling before they can run you too need to be ok with this in all areas of your life. Growing up is essential to your next step. 1 Corinthians 13:11 shows us how we put childlike ways behind us in order to walk in new love.

CHAPTER SIX

Pause Effect

If you're anything like me after I have taken a few steps in the right direction for whatever crazy reason I find myself at a halt. No matter what it may be if your girl is wanting to get somewhere, I get in this pause button effect. It's like I forget that I am on a journey and don't know which way to go. It's my crossroads, it's my middle of transition, it's that wait one-minute place. This place is bigger than I realize. I did not know how dangerous this place could be. The pause effect is about wasting time, energy, purpose. It's when we lose a moment and forget which way we are going. If you're like me this can be all too familiar but don't worry let me help you get unstuck.

When we lack vision, we perish. I remember being in bible school and my pastor teaching us that very truth. Without vision the people perish. We don't know which way we are going and what in the world we are doing. Not only is vision for your life important it's most important in this season. What causes the pause effect, lack of vision and lack of discipline. The pause effect causes us to do one thing that keeps us from the vision. Waste time! Are you wasting time. Have you gotten to a place where you're just standing in a four way stop not knowing which way to go next.

I've been there and my wasted time was not just time it was a waste of energy, sleep, and peace. It was a waste of everything. I found myself spinning in circles following everyone and everything but my purpose. To be honest I can't even blame anyone but myself. I allowed my love for others and things to keep my eyes off the vision. Have you ever been in the middle of a great movie or book then the power goes out or someone knocks on the door. You hit rock bottom, walk away and not come back to it until days later because whatever caught your attention took you off the routine of what you already had going on. Yep that was me. I had allowed myself to hit the pause button and miss out on the rest of the story I was trying to finish.

Do you find yourself at times forgetting what your vision is? Maybe the new year started, and you made a vision board but tell me where it is? You stated the year with great baby steps then what? What happened to the vision? Or maybe you know that you're in a relationship that's wasting your time and you need to leave but instead of walking away you stay put why? Why are you wasting your time and energy knowing you deserve more.

I urge you to re-shift your focus. The world needs you! Yes you! We need your ideas, your voice. Your talent God did not give us the diaries in our hearts for us to get stuck and not continually pursue the things of him, I don't expect you to be perfect because that would have to be an expectation I put on myself and I am so far from a perfect person. But one thing I refuse to be is someone who lets her dreams pass her by because I chose to waste time. No longer are we going to waste our lives not chasing our dreams. So, no matter what it is you're reading this book for, don't be controlled by the pause effect. Take back control of your life and hit that play button! Start dreaming and believing again. Take a moment to write down who is it you want to be? And what are you doing to keep up the momentum, so you don't waste time.

Who do I want to be?

What am I doing to get there?

Am I suck?

CHAPTER SEVEN
Surrender

What does surrender mean?
When I think of surrendering, I felt like I am defeated. Like I have lost that very thing I have been fighting for. But man was I wrong about this. My Mindset of what it meant to truly trust God was all out of whack. Yes, I said trust why? Because lack of surrender comes from lack of trust. I wish I could tell you that trusting is the easiest thing to do in the book. But who am I kidding one thing I will never be to you is a liar. I know from experience that there is power in my testimony and in just being flat out real. Like come on folks we know our generation strives to have the real given to us all the time. Even though somehow, we still end up being really fake but that's just a side note. Anyway, let's get on track, learning what it means to surrender means learning what it means to close your eyes. stand on the edge of a cliff and just fall back. Now I don't mean this in a literal sense but in all deposits a figurative one. Have you ever been at a point in your life where you just felt like you need to take a leap of faith or might as well let go because there's no point in holding on? Well that my friends is the perfect place to be when

getting ready to seek surrender. The actual definition of surrender means to sense resistance to an enemy or opponent and submit to an authority. Now if this does not get you all shook up in your bones then maybe you're not seeking true change. I find it funny how submission comes with surrender.

When we learn to submit our lives into God's hand, we then can learn to surrender our fears and plans to him. One of my favorite songs as a child was, he got the whole world in his hands. It brought me comfort knowing that God had everything in my life in the palm of his hands. It brought me peace knowing that I did not have to stress about what will happen to the world Because God got it. Well it's the same in my life I had to get to a place where I know that God got me. He got my life in his hands and I only need to fall back and trust him.

This may be the hardest part for some of you. A trust fall is no simple thing, especially if you don't trust the person you are falling back on. But know that when you're ready and you do just fall without thinking about it, he will catch you and he will hold you. When you allow yourself to get out of your head and allow your life to be lived to the fullest taking every risk, failing forward, learning and growing from every mistake then oh then will the submission and surrender bring forth the courage you need to reshape your life.

CHAPTER EIGHT
Reshape

After defining what it means to be His beloved and talking about the ups and downs that have occurred in our lives. Moving forward means taking a deeper look into reshaping. If you have yet to understand your value or have found yourself frozen in time, then this is an important lesson. Reshaping is about self-love not only physically but spiritually and mentally as well. No matter your reason for reading this book you will entail remembering that this season is about you. Loving you. Finding you, understanding you, all about you. So reshaping is simply remembering what this whole journey is about. What does it mean to be loved? Love is in so many ways defined but the greatest love we can have outside of loving Christ is loving self. The tricky thing is self-love can also become self-distraction if not careful. What do I mean? Well we are meant to love us first to then be an extension. Love is meant to be filled to an overflow where we mess up if we love on empty or we love and never pour out.

Reshaping begins with the understanding of who we are intended to be. Vessels! We are created to carry and carry with abundance. So how can I reshape and become the abundance I am? It starts in the mind. Romans 12:2 teaches us the importance of transforming our minds. Not only do we need to shift the way we think but we need to use it to test God's will for our lives. Brothers and sisters don't let the world be the thing that defines who you are. You are created to live out a life that God set out for you and it is perfect and pleasing.

This season of self-love is not one that only comes once in your lifetime but one that circles around in every season of your life. Lately God has shown me and put this so heavy on my heart that you have to reshape and redefine who you are in every season. Your single season is meant for you to find and be your best self just you and the Lord. But as a husband or a wife that self is no longer just about you. You have to redefine what self looks like with another person. Your purpose for your missions now is entangled with someone else. It's no longer your dreams but our dreams. I am not saying there is not a strength and beauty in it all, I am saying each season is a reshaping. So, if you're not growing, we need to reevaluate where we are and look back on some baby steps that we may have missed. Reshaping is one of the most important stages in your growth, you're no longer looking in the lens of who you one were but in the lenses of who you now are. You are not your past, you are not who you used to be , the person you are in this season is your best you , your better you, your stronger you and that person needs to be loved as much as you loved the younger version of yourself.

Yes, reshaping is hard. I don't know much about pottery making but when I see that clay get folded up and bent any time to create it's perfect masterpiece it takes lots of effort and lots of water which I see as guiding grace to reshape and bend the clay into its next stage. Just like we spoke about in baby steps the pain from falling and the pain from our muscles growing into its next stage is the same way it is now in shifting our minds to love ourselves in this new season. Can it be a challenge yes however the outcome of it all is so worth it. The joy we gain loving your best self, your better self is what elevates you into the next level, it's how you truly find your beloved.

CHAPTER NINE
Reverse the curse

I don't know if during your journey of reading you guessed or figured out that I am a Christian. If you have not caught on to that it's totally cool, no harm or foul taken. I am though in fact a Christian and proud to say it. The reason I'm even telling you this is because it's who I am, it's my identity, it's who I am proud to be. And like I have been teaching you and speaking to you about in the past chapters is truly falling in love with you, whoever you are. Finding your best self and loving it in every season of your life. Remember when we feel less than we need to reshape our thoughts and our actions. Last chapter I spoke to you about some of the pain I have faced in my life. I hope my story is of encouragement to you, and helps you overcome your burdens. This next challenge is like the others' deep heart searching for huge deliverance and freedom.

If you don't know this girl did not grow up in church. Well I did not but really. my family grew up catholic and went to mass Sundays here and there. It was honestly good for the most part there was so much beauty in the catholic church that I feel like other churches miss out on. However, there was still something missing for me. There was a deepness in my heart that was still longing for more. There was something I just had to find that would answer all my questions and fill all my voids. It took me until I was about 15 to feel like I found the answer to my questions. In the simplest and most unexpected way, my answer was my faith. My love in Christ helped grow my love in self. Why? Because God created us all and no one loves their baby more than its creator. In this season as you're creating the best you are falling in love with that very same you. Well the one who created you into this world that's how he feels about you daily. To see the very thing, he created grow into the best of its abilities is so fulfilling.

Many of you may be like me, we come from hard stories, crazy backgrounds. We have seen pain in so many forms and have experienced many hard days, let me encourage you, you have the power to reverse the curse. I mentioned to you my story of my faith because for me that was my way in finding my truth, in falling in love with the creator to know how to love me. In order to do so we have to dig deeper and allow ourselves to explore some of the deeper issues we are facing and that is part of the next step in understanding the hidden truths in our lives.

CHAPTER TEN
The Hidden Truth

It is easy for us to talk about all the good things in our lives. The things that make us happy or the accomplishments we have gained. But where does the truth lie in all of that? What is your hidden truth? If we are being honest with each other we can all say it was the hard times that shaped us into who we are now. We use the phrase "what does not kill us makes us stronger" though I find that to be true in my life there is also a scripture I like to lean into as well. "I can do all things through Christ who strengthens me." You see, what makes the pain turn into strength is all perspective. How are you viewing your hardships?

My life has many hidden truths. It's not just about the moments in which my heart felt broken about old relationships, it's about every detail of my life. I am sure if we were sitting face to face right now having this conversation that even in your life you have had many situations that have been hardships for you as well. So, let dig into that and let's have this hidden truth conversation. I would start the question off by asking who are you? Wait one minute remember we are talking about the real you the you that people don't see on the surface. Who are you really? Maybe this question may be hard for some of you to explain or even think about. Maybe for some of you, you never stopped to look inside yourself to find who you really are. Well that's ok this is why we are on this journey together. So, let's take that moment and ask ourselves the question: who am I really? If you need to put this book down and evaluate please do so and let the holy spirit speak to your memories and find all the details in who you are.

Like many defining who I am was no easy task. It took me time. It took me moments of pain to look back into my life and see the things that shaped me into the person that I am now. For me what shaped me was not all joy and happy moments but pain and traumatic moments where I found myself saying I never want to be like that. My hidden truth is that from a very young age I saw abuse and I saw pain. From my father being verbally and physically abusive to being exposed to porn and sex at a very young age. So many different things became a part of my story and became a part of who I was. My trauma went from childhood into adulthood. I felt like it was one trauma after the other. Never getting a grip of freedom. Little did I know this hidden part of me helped build me up. Now hear me, I am not saying that you need to have trauma in your life. What I am saying is that trauma does not define you but only shapes you. It's all about perspective.

Understanding who you are, trauma or not, is essential. This becomes the push and foundation to who you will be. In this season many of us are redefining who we are. We have listened to this voice in our heads for so long saying we can't, we will never be, we are not good enough, but in this season, we will not allow what is in the dark to keep us bound. One story I love in the bible is the story of Jacob. Most people only see him as the man who stole his brother's birthrights and then ran away. Yes, that's all true in who he was, but what I love most about his story all lies in one chapter. Chapter 32 the moment where his life changed forever. If we look closely to this chapter, we see two very important things: one we see how he wrestles with God and like many of us we too can say we have wrestled with God concerning us. So, he wrestles with God and then God touches him. He breaks him and in that moment his life is forever changed. I don't know about you but when I am broken before God my life is forever changed but also in more detail when God touches me, I am forever changed. Jacob was broken and he would no longer ever walk the same. When we do the same in our lives, I promise you will no longer walk the same after a touch from heaven. So here Jacob is broken and forever changed, and you would think that was more than enough for God, but no God had bigger plans for him God saw more in him. So not only did he change him but redefined him, all with one simple question. Who are you? At that moment this question would changes Jacob's life forever. Who are you? A question filled with so much power, so much pain, so much destiny. Jacob the man who had been lying, stealing and cheating from his own family had to have a moment to dig deep and expose all his hidden truth. He had to bring to light the real him the real story. I am sure in that moment it was not easy for him to say I am Jacob not just meaning his name but also meaning everything he was and did. I am sure after already being broken to say that on top of it all was hard, but it was in that moment his life shifted in that moment God moved for him.

God saw the real him and spoke to him and said you will no longer be Jacob but be my promise. God took who he was and redefined him. No, he did not wake up a different person, but he woke up with a different perspective.

So, who are you? Before we can work on shifting our perspective and redefining our lives, answer to yourself who you really are. And I pray and believe with all the faith that I have that in this struggle in this season God will redefine who you are and you will walk into your purpose but first let's get real with one another and expose all the hidden truths we have kept away from the light.

CHAPTER ELEVEN
Birthing

I hear the birthing room is one special type of place. Now when I say special, I don't mean anything fancy, I have seen hospital rooms far too many times to know there isn't anything that's cool or cozy about that place. Unless maybe you have had some nice first classroom and that place my friends, I have never seen. Any one back on track. So, yea there is this room where all women have to go into in order to give birth. Yes, the rooms may all have different things in them however there are a few factors that remain the same. Now I know some of you may be thinking where she is even going with this. Here me out because this really has nothing to do with actual birth, because your girl doesn't even have actual kids yet.

This is about who you have in our circle in this season. This is your birthing season. So, I can't speak about birth in a literal sense because like I just mentioned I have not yet experienced the pains of childbirth. However, the spiritual in many ways reflects the natural. And though I may not yet have had a natural birth, I have in many seasons had to birth new things spiritually. In fact, this book is part of that birthing process. And though I don't have a baby that cries all night, this is my baby and I have cried all night bringing it into this world. So, how does this connect with who is in your circle, I am glad you asked.

Let's look at what a typical birthing room consists of. A doctor, the person who is leading the show, nurses the second in command but also the ones who are encouraging you since they know what they are doing. Then you have the father, the one who is closest to you in this process because he is connected to what comes out of you. Then we have a close family member or friend. Then you of course we can't forget ourselves. So, that is the whole scene of five very valuable people in the middle of a great shift in life. Why is this set up so important? This setup is a part of the process in which we are all in and it's also one of the most important to understand.

We have all come a long way from the beginning of this journey understanding who we are, setting reality up for our best outcomes, taking the steps to grow, we been doing it all. If you have not stopped to reflect on where you have come from and see that even in the little things how you have grown, then please take a moment to do that. Look at how far you have carried yourself from. Are you perfect now? No, but you have overcome, you have beat what you thought would tear you down, you forgave and healed from pain. You have grown and you need to recognize that. It's ok if you are not where you want to be, but you are not where you used to be and that's worth celebrating.

    You have carried this baby, this growth of yourself in you, and now it is time to transition into being the new version of you. so, it's important that in that transition we take time to check our surroundings and make sure we are setting ourselves up with the right people around us. If you're anything like me this may be the hardest step for you, I'm here to tell you that's ok it's hard for me too. It's hard because you are evaluating who is really for you and who is not. If you are used to having people in your life all the time, it's going to feel very uncomfortable but if you're used to being on your own it's going to mean seeking out others to be there for you as well. Not everyone is meant for this moment, not everyone can handle the pain and ugly parts of birth. But know that the closest people to you, the people you invite into that delivery room are the people who cherish you most and understand the pain that came with birthing this baby like none other.

    Let's take a deep look into who is who. If you have not already guessed it God is the doctor. He is the man running this show. He is the one who *has performed miracle after miracle in our lives and knows what to do and when to do it. Then we got our number one champ of a nurse who is right there with the doc. Been through it all, seen it all, Jesus and the Holy spirit. Our advocate and person we lean on to help us with pretty much everything. Your nurse becomes your best friend. Ask any of your mama friends they all pray to have a great nurse in their room and that's for a reason, we need the best of the best. Now this is the part that gets challenging really knowing who's who is when it comes to the family members. Naturally you may want it to be a whole lot of people because you want others to feel included or apart. I know for me this is my issue. I know what it feels like being shut out or feeling less than, so I work hard to make sure others don't feel like that, because my heart is to make others happy, I forget the importance of what's best for Ashley. Deciding who I have as my cheerleader in this delivery process is very critical. Why? Because not everyone is for you! Let's repeat not everyone is for you!*

I know for me I want to think the best about people, I want to believe that people see and give love the same way I do. News flash they do not! just because you love and give of yourself does not mean they all will do the same for you. Wanna test it, don't call that so called friend for a week and see if they call you, or how about stop driving two hours every weekend to see people and see who comes to see you, now don't base it off what they say either, because people sure do love to say they are here for you or they will come see you but then leave you in the dust waiting on them to appear and you never see them. What I'm saying is don't be like me guys, I truly have spent so much energy pouring out on others that are not here right now. Even as I type this book out, I am exhausted in this birthing season because the people I poured into thinking would be the ones wiping the tears and sweat away are the ones that are nowhere to be found. But out there living and doing what they wanna do. So, let me save you from all this pain and heartache that I am walking through.

    The father is someone or something you believe your miracle is tied to. Don't get stuck on thinking it has to be a person because that's not true. It could be your calling or a dream. This book is not attached to my husband but is attached to you. This miracle was born to be a blessing to you and me both. So, remember the father is not always a person, but if it is a person or persons evaluate their value in this miracle. Then we have our *closest friend or family. Now I know some people have more than one person outside of the father show up for this great but hard time but for me I don't want any more than two people there in this situation. One! let's be real birthing is beautiful but also very messy and vulnerable and not everyone is meant to see you naked. And two not everyone will understand. So, I'll do what the bible says and stick to the two or three that gather, because I know Jesus is there and that's all I can handle anyway. So, the people who you pick as your closet people, are you sure they are that. Your closest may look different than mine, but what I know is that they are not the ones that I am questioning if they are for me or not. They are not the ones I have to beg to show up for me, or to pray for me, they're the ones who have already seen me at my worst and have loved me through it. There the ones that God forbid anything to happen to me they would know how to take care of this miracle and let it continue to live on. These are very important people!*

God gave me this birthing analogy because he knew I would need it in such a time as this. He knew you would need it to check who is in your birthing room. However, I can't leave out the most important person in this room. That's right you!

No one and I repeat no one is feeling what you're feeling, no one knows how much this hurts for you to birth this promise into the world. No one knows all the hard work that went behind getting to this point. The thoughts you had to overcome, the things you had to shift, the people you had to let go. However, no one knows how amazing it is to be you. You are birthing a part of you into the world. You are creating a new life. Whether that is literal or just figurative you are in fact bringing something new to the world that has never been here before. There is only one you and only one person can create what's about to come. So, listen, this is about you! It always has been till the end.

However these people are important to this moment you need them, you need God more than you think you do, so stop trying to fight him and listen to what he is saying because he knows what he is doing more than you do, talk to the Holy Spirit tell him what your needs and fears are. Look at the Father and know that this is as much for them as it is for you and rely on your cheerleaders because they are with you to keep you going. But just like real birth it's ok to yell it's ok to scream it's ok to ask for what you need to make it through this. Be all the messy things you need to be in order to bring this message into the world but do just that! Birth it, don't let it die, don't give up, don't quit, keep going and push, push, push the miracle you have had in you into the world.

CHAPTER TWELVE

Be-Loved

Many of the stories and lessons that have appeared here have taught me and I pray have taught you a great deal of lessons in maximizing this season you are in. I would like to highlight the important facts of becoming who you are in this season you are in .and understanding that now is your time for greatness and more.

This journey is about finding yourself, being whole and connected to your true purpose while holding onto the promises that God has given you and working towards becoming the best at your craft in the meantime. We are taking the baby steps to let go of our false reality and brokenness that we have been walking in for far too long. this journey is to help us surrender and reshape our minds, hearts, and life back to God. The truth is, it's only until then we will see the fullness of our season and only then will we unveil the hidden truth and cures we have struggled with for years. Your journey is to grow into your best to birth into the world a new and better version of you. so, we understand how to be-love. To be loved is to be whole within who you are. We spoke once before how beloved two words is and is simply placed in one. be and loved. be who you are, be who you are created to be. be happy, be whole, be free from the lies. be creative, be fun, be spontaneous. be kind, be wild, be something new. the key to being a beloved is simply being and becoming. When you grab a hold of that truth then loving becomes so much easier. When you love who you are becoming, you got it, when you love who you are being you got it. When you know that you are love in this very season of your life then you are his beloved. you are the most important thing to God. and you are important to this world. I pray that you have seen and understood that along this journey. I pray you have reflected on the worth you bring to with world. And that you know you are made for greatness and you are worth the wait of this season until someone see you for who you really are. My beloved is you. My being is having the opportunity to say to you that you are oh so loved. that this season is the best season for growth. that soon and very soon someone too will see you for who you are and love you too. Don't rush out of this season without loving who you are to its fullness. Don't take on another relationship until you know how to be loved.

I leave you here with this one last task, a prayer. as you read and pray this prayer over yourself, I pray it ministers to you. I pray it breaks down walls and chains. I pray that you are no longer the same after this moment. if you like you can speak this prayer out loud in a privet place, so it also becomes your prayer.

Dear God. I thank you for today. I thank you for allowing me this opportunity to speak into your child's life. I thank you that at this very moment you are here with us. God, I come to you today to ask you for your healing. heal our hearts, minds, and bodies from all things not of you. God reverse the cures off of our lives, Lord help us to not live in a false idea of what it means to be your beloved. Help us to live according to your will and word. Lord I ask you for your guidance and for the strength. And help me to continue taking baby steps in the right direction. While helping me to birth your promises for my life into the world. yes, God at times it is very hard but with your help I can overcome anything. so, I ask you again Lord please help me become your beloved and birth truth., thank you for treasuring me and calling me your own. help me to wait until the right person can see me as you do before calling me their own. I honor and praise you in Jesus name. -amen.

CONCLUSION

Wow just wow. I am so proud of you for walking along side me on this journey. I hope you have gained a better understanding of this season. and that you are now walking away stronger than when you came in. My beloved you are worth more the precious jewels (Prov. 31 v:10)

You are made to be-loved by the right person in the right season, and after this season you will have clarity in how to do so. Go and change the world with who you are, overcome thoughts hard things in your life. this is now your beginning of becoming a beloved.

For Booking and Speaking Engagements

Contact: Ashley Ikwueme

Phone: 706-610-0709

FB: Ashley Ikwm

Personal Blog: Anchored in Me

https: Linktr.ee//Anchoredim

Made in the USA
Columbia, SC
17 December 2020